BASIC SECURITY FUNDAMENTALS

2nd Edition

C. R. JAHN

AUTHOR'S NOTE

A substantial portion of this book was originally commissioned as a training manual for a local security firm. Very good, practical, solid information here that can benefit all entry level security officers, supervisors, and managers as well as clients considering hiring a uniformed guard patrol service. The manual is presented in its complete form with additional material.

This book will describe the various types of domestic entry level security employment available, as well as different types of employer, posts, and duties. You will be given tips on ways to make your job safer and easier, as well as hard earned advice on what types of job to avoid and why.

I have over 30 years of experience working with a number of security and investigations firms in three states. I have personally worked dozens of contracts under a variety of circumstances and have observed a lot. These observations, as well as advice for anyone considering choosing a security firm to work for, have been added.

1. INTRODUCTION:

Hello. My name is C.R. Jahn and I am the author of numerous titles regarding the topic of self defense. My career in the security industry permitted me opportunity to pursue writing, by providing a steady paycheck as well as plenty of time to write while on the job. Security typically provides an abundance of free time, if you select a graveyard shift detail.

I have over 30 years of experience in security and investigations, in multiple capacities in several states. There is a very wide spectrum of security work available, and every firm has its own expectations, challenges, and culture. I will explore these differences in my own unique style, which, if you are familiar with my other works, tends to be coarse and occasionally peppered with profanity. If that offends you, I apologize, but it is what it is. Security attracts a plethora of personality types, from the very best to the very worst. All are treated equally: with ambivalence and miserable pay.

The thing you need to understand is that security is widely considered an unskilled entry level job, and you will be paid and treated accordingly. This can be a good thing as well as a bad thing. For one, the employer's expectations will generally be reasonable and low. They will be ever so happy if you arrive on site, on time, in your uniform, and perform the bare minimum patrol and reporting tasks while causing no problems. It is a HUGE red flag if an employer expects significantly more than this, because all security jobs pay about the same, typically with no benefits and zero chance of raises or promotion. But on the other hand, guards are thought of as "temporary labor" and easily replaced. Guards are terminated all the time for very minor cause or no cause. Similarly, contracts are canceled and entire firms are fired by clients, often due to spurious or false cause, simply because a competing firm offered to perform the same job cheaper while claiming to be able to do it "better." Perhaps they even can, but in the long run there seldom is much loyalty to firms or individual guards and it usually comes down to how much the client can "save" on the bottom line at the end of each quarter.

Security is GREAT for a responsible adult who would be satisfied working a relatively undemanding job for low pay. The average hourly wage for a security guard is between $10 and $13. Any place that offers less pay is to be avoided, and any place that offers more pay typically either is a government job with stiff competition for the limited positions available (health care benefits and paid sick days are great incentives to apply for a job at a university or library, but high stress due to unrealistic expectations contributes to high turnover), or they are armed positions which requires additional training and certification. You want to avoid any armed security work that pays under $15 per hour. Remember, whatever you are being paid, the firm is typically being paid double that by the client, which largely goes to cover the expenses of an office and vehicles... so if your employer has neither an office or vehicles, they are keeping their expenses low. Typically armed security is expected to stand on their feet all shift to supposedly scare potential robbers, but they just shoot the guard first, usually in the back of the head. We have an armored car service here that pays only $12 an hour, and you need to buy your own gun and vest. Smaller firms with smaller budgets will often advertise for applicants who "have their own duty gear" and that is fine if you have it and they are up front about it. You need to avoid any firm that expects you to pay for your own uniform though. That is actually illegal under the Labor Law. Additionally, with limited exceptions, you should avoid any firm that does not provide uniforms, especially if it is low paying and outdoors. That uniform identifies you as someone who is supposed to be there and has lawful right to confront trespassers, so if you are not provided a uniform it is in your best interest to purchase a shirt that says SECURITY so people don't think you're a mugger or something when they run into you after dark.

You do not want to have graveyard shift patrol duties and no uniform. Some clients do not want you in uniform, believing it is "unwelcoming" or does not fit their image, and that is fine. I worked two jobs like that, a Lexus dealership and a mental health crisis center. For those positions I simply wore a navy blue Dickies work shirt, which resembles a uniform. When patrolling outdoors after dark, I would clip a security badge to my belt (purchased from eBay) and turn on the broadcastify scanner app on my phone. This presented both a visual and audio message that I was working security and not a trespasser or thief, yet I still got the police called on me at least twice a year anyway. If you confront someone without any indication you are authorized to do so, they are far more likely to view you as a threat than a deterrent. The scanner noise made me appear more "official" and also served to "bell the cat," letting trespassers know I was approaching so they would have opportunity to hide or retreat and would not be startled into violence... and if you are being paid under $12 an hour with no health insurance you are not being compensated nearly enough to fight tweakers or arrest hobos. All legitimate security training emphasizes that your primary duty is simply to "observe and report."

2. TYPES OF SECURITY DETAIL

That brings me to my next point: "tactical" security firms. While notable exceptions do exist, as a general rule you want to avoid these firms like the plague. I know a lot of guys who are former military special ops, and they disparagingly refer to these inept clowns as "tacticool" poseurs or Walter Mittys. Allow me to explain. First and foremost, the owner seems to be living out a fantasy, if not a delusion, that he is some sort of paramilitary badass his "team" (always a "team", although guards invariably work alone) should emulate. He will insist his guards wear black boots and black military style BDU trousers with tactical black jackets that have velcro on the sleeves for attaching patches. These are usually unarmed positions, in that no sidearm is permitted, but they will want guards to wear a duty belt loaded down with a baton, Mace, Mag-Lite, and 2 pairs of handcuffs. Frequently they will expect guards to purchase these things, or deduct a "deposit" for them from their first paycheck. These firms often send their guards into high risk environments, such as low income housing units or bus stations, and encourage them to "make arrests" with zero training in proper use of the baton or the legalities of use of force, with absolutely no backup or radio contact with a dispatcher. You would be expected to intervene in domestic disputes and burglaries in progress... calls that armed and experienced policemen refuse to roll on without backup. To top things off, they invariably pay less than industry standard... I think the "tactical" guard at the local Greyhound terminal makes $9 an hour and is expected to "make at least 2 arrests every shift." This is the very definition of a high risk, low reward job. Each of these employers assured me that they "had my back" regarding legal defense should I ever find myself in court as the result of a use of force incident, yet refused to put that guarantee in writing.

Do not trust these clowns one bit, even when it comes to being reimbursed for expenses or getting paid overtime. You will be lucky if you see a pay stub itemized with deductions. Very unprofessional.

Even worse than the tacticool "teams" is loss prevention. These are jobs where you are expected to arrest thieves in plain clothes and escort them back to the security office until police arrive. If you are physically intimidating with a professional demeanor, this is usually uneventful 90% of the time. The other times, you may need to fight a suspect, or even multiple suspects, who may be armed with knives or Mace or even a gun... whereas loss prevention is invariably unarmed due to "liability." You will face regular accusations of "excessive force" even when no force was used, or even sexual molestation of female shoplifters, which is why most stores have cameras in the security office as well as a policy that a female employee must be present during the arrest as a witness. And if you arrest a minor, frequently the parents will show abject hostility towards you. You need to be able to document a recording of the suspect actually concealing merchandise on their person to have a solid case, but many smaller stores lack that capability, and you may be accused of false arrest, unlawful imprisonment, and additional charges related to searching their person if no merchandise is found. Far greater potential for injury and litigation with loss prevention than most other security jobs, and again, low pay and nonexistent benefits. Again, even if management "has your back," corporate does not. If an arrestee threatens to sue, expect to be thrown under the bus. Very high turnover in loss prevention jobs.

Nightclub security is a bit of a step up. The environment is fun and you will get to be indoors, sitting around listening to music and watching scantily clad drunk women gyrating on the dance floor. You also, very likely, will have at least several other security personnel backing you up, with whom you remain in constant communication via radio. However, the type of clubs vary, as do the patrons and their behaviors. Strip clubs are generally considered to be the worst, in terms of incidents and safety. Many gang members, drug dealers, and pimps patronize these establishments, frequently in possession of weapons while under the influence, which is why there often are metal detectors at the door and the doorman usually is armed with a high caliber handgun. These drunk, coke fueled, armed criminals will come into contact with White, middle class, affluent citizens, who are also drunk. Your job is to prevent the wealthy yet naive customers from being jumped, beaten, and robbed. These incidents usually occur outside in the parking lot. Next to strip clubs, hip hop clubs, Latin clubs, Country Western bars, biker bars, and Jazz/Blues bars are considered to have the most potential for serious violence... however, sports bars and college bars invariably have the highest number of incidents involving drunken belligerence. Be advised that drunk people are annoying and problematic, but drugged up people are worse, especially people who have progressed beyond recreational use into addiction. Wherever tweakers and cokeheads congregate, there will be crime: robbery, theft, fraud, prostitution, sale of stolen goods, and of course drug dealing. You will need to be very observant as well as careful to abide by the policies of management with common sense, but without alienating regular customers or neighbors. You will occasionally need to fight people in this job, but without seriously injuring them. This job is not for everyone.

Next we have details posted at universities and hospitals. These tend to be fairly cushy jobs, being indoors in well maintained buildings with few serious incidents. Your primary focus will be on the occasional fire alarm evacuation. In the event that a student, patient, or visitor becomes escalated and begins making threats or actually physically assaulting people, do not be surprised if you are immediately terminated for attempting to stop them. You see, most academics and doctors live in a bubble of privilege that also serves as an echo chamber of virtue signaling. You need to understand that they view you as a "wannabe cop" who is "a dime a dozen" and violence is the worst thing ever. Indeed, there may be written policy dictating that you may never place hands on an assaultive person or even raise your voice while telling him NO. Or, even worse, there may be no set policy and administrators simply make up new rules at their whim. Regardless, expect to be judged relentlessly everyday and subject to regular anonymous passive-aggressive complaints that you may hear of third or fourth hand with no opportunity to contest them or even offer an explanation. See above where you are "a dime a dozen." Perhaps you failed to smile wide enough or offer a sufficiently enthusiastic greeting when one of these egotistical cretins walked past and they decided you needed to be "put in your place" for that transgression. But if you are naturally cheerful, unoffensive, and compulsively apologetic, there may be a long term position available for you here.

Shopping mall details are one of the worst. Like Rodney Dangerfield, you literally have no respect. Teenaged kids love fucking with the mall cops, thinking "You aren't allowed to touch me!" and in many cases they are actually right. Typically, the bigger and fancier the mall, the more worried they are about "liability" and "customer relations." That means, like a typical university or hospital detail, you will likely be forbidden to carry a pocketknife, let alone a duty belt with Mace, baton, and cuffs. Many mall cops spend most of their shift driving around a vast parking lot in a dirty broke ass vehicle with a yellow flashing light on top, supposedly to serve as a "deterrent." They run the gambit from the guy who fails to notice the car with the dead body in the front seat that has been parked there for a month, to the super cop who wants to arrest teenagers for making out in their parked car. This is a awful job, which attracts awful people, and you will eat the Cinnabon and weep. Strip malls in the ghetto are different. You will probably get a Taser and Mace and will deal with crackheads all day... and their crackhead families, which always include a brood of screaming brats. You will be expected to quell disruptions as well as arrest shoplifters. How much do you think this job pays? About the same as a boring night watchman position where you are paid not to sleep.

Event security usually entails checking for tickets and weapons at the front door, which is easy peasy, but you are on your feet for hours, usually standing in the same place, and it is raining. People will get angry when asked to open purses and backpacks, and you will need to tell people "NO" and "That's just the way it is" a lot. Event security staff is hated almost as much as the molesters at TSA. Every venue is different. Many are a free for all inside and a bloodbath out in the parking lot because security never leaves the front doors. Some details will expect you to patrol indoors, looking for fights and checking the restroom for perverts. You may be expected to deny access to off limits or VIP areas. You may be expected to patrol the parking lots during the show. All of these extra duties should involve additional pay, but usually they do not. The guy at one venue who gets to sit on a stool out of the rain and tell Facebook it is wrong for 5 hours usually gets paid the same as the schmuck breaking up fights and confronting thieves breaking into cars, so be certain what you're getting into. Some venues even allow you to enjoy the show for free, which is a nice bonus

Hotel security is an interesting job. It is primarily indoors, with a couple patrols of the parking area. Your job is to patrol the corridors and respond to complaints. 90% of these complaints are about another guest being too noisy. Every weekend you will need to deal with drunk guests in accordance with hotel policy, and you will need to keep out drunks who are not guests. You will occasionally have drug dealers and prostitutes operating out of a room and will be expected to notify police if their activities become too obvious. There will be thefts from rooms, drug overdoses, suicides, domestic abuse, and rapes. It is serious, responsible work, and you will be expected to wear a blazer and tie, and be articulate and courteous, as well as discrete. You will be in contact with local law enforcement regularly and may be expected to make the occasional arrest. Certainly not a job for everyone, but has the potential for longterm employment and job satisfaction.

Office buildings and high rise condos have various levels of security and access control. A "concierge" position basically has you sit at a desk all shift, smile pleasantly, give directions and accept deliveries. Hardly an actual "security" job at all, more like customer service. Other buildings have strict access control requirements. You will be responsible for issuing and accounting for keys, access cards, and access fobs. These will need to be programmed and logged, often in exchange for a driver license or other identification card. Cleaning staff, contractors, vendors, and guests all need to go through this process. This job typically involves monitoring CCTV camera monitors for most of your shift, and it is important to present a professional appearance and demeanor. Great if you don't mind saying "sir" a lot and sitting at a desk all day. Relatively low stress job.

Gated communities usually do not have guards, instead relying upon a key card or access code for tenants to enter, but a few actually have a guard shack to check authorized guests and contractors against a list. Typically you remain in the guard shack all day. Dealing with spoiled rich people is worse than dealing with the hobos... some of them act like lizard people from another planet. You will be expected to smile a lot, make inane small talk all day, and memorize everyone's name. The rich people will think nothing of walking into the guard shack unannounced, with their little yappy dog, to make comments on the weather or interrogate you regarding personal matters, because they "pay your salary." Some people love this type of detail, and on the overnight shift it is usually very slow.

Transportation security deals with the trucking industry, and you should have familiarity and comfort with the trucking culture. You will need to be polite and respectful, yet firm. Most truckers are decent people, and are worried that an incident might cost them their job and perhaps their CDL... others, not so much... and a few will show up drunk or on meth. This is a straight up blue collar job and you need to be tough. You will be logging trucks in and out, weighing them on scales, and patrolling outdoors in all sorts of weather. Some yards are open 24 hours, whereas others have gates that are closed and locked at certain times. You will be expected to regularly tell large angry men "NO" and occasionally even bang on the side of their truck in the middle of the night to wake them up. In some cases, you may be working at a trainyard instead of a trucking yard, and that is much easier for the most part, except that you will need to look out for hobos riding in open boxcars and tweakers trying to break into locked ones. Some very nasty characters ride the rails, including the violent criminal gang FTRA and many dangerous fugitives. Serial killers have ridden the rails. These evil people frequently victimize the harmless hippies and runaways simply looking for a free ride and are usually armed, often with framing hammers or padlocks swung from bandannas. For shelter, you will typically have a tiny 6X6 guard shack with a fan in the Summer and a space heater in the Winter. Embrace the suck. Surprisingly, this often pays better than most other unarmed security details.

Industrial security is basically a night watchman position combined with firewatch duties. You will be expected to make several patrols a night and may be exposed to unsafe hazardous conditions as well as toxic chemicals, dust, or fumes. You will typically need to check pressure gauges on various pieces of equipment and telephone an engineer if a gauge reads too low or too high. You will be looking for fires and burglars. It is not a particularly bad job, unless the conditions at the site are unusually bad. Patrolling in the mud and snow with only a flashlight to guide you is not fun, and the pay is shit. The guard shack at most industrial sites is usually a bit larger and better equipped than at transportation sites.

Night watchman jobs can be at a variety of settings: construction sites, parking garages, historic properties. Basically, you are expected to stay awake all night and call police if you spot a burglar or vandal. This is known as "make money while you sleep" in the security industry, because that is what half of all guards assigned to these details do. Or they drink whiskey and jerk off. Basically, this is a job for drunks and jerk offs who cannot be trusted with greater responsibility. You typically are expected to drive to the site and shelter in your personal vehicle. This is great fun in the Wintertime, burning your own gas all night to stay warm. There is seldom an electric outlet on site you can run an extension cord to, lights, or even a port-a-john. This is considered bottom of the barrel, but it is not without its charm. If there is light available you can read books. If there is an outlet available you can use a laptop to watch movies or do schoolwork... I wrote several books while employed as a night watchman, which in many ways is a lot better than applying for a National Endowment for the Arts grant. A few guys I knew watched streaming movies from Netflix on their phone all night, which destroys your night vision but whatever. It is a VERY boring job, but you rarely need to interact with humanity, which is a bonus. These jobs typically pay about 10 bucks an hour.

Fire watch is rock bottom. You are literally paid to stare at a construction site, or maybe some haystacks or a giant pile of sawdust, and call 911 if you see smoke or fire. Again, you'll be using your own vehicle for shelter, but likely will not be expected to patrol. These jobs are typically claimed by frail elderly men well past retirement age. Uniforms are seldom issued or required. Presence of a fire watch person is mandated by insurance companies or local fire code at some facilities where spontaneous combustion is a risk. Pay is even less than night watchman, typically only 8 or 9 bucks an hour, and the client will treat you like a retard. You do not want this job.

3. WORKING THE JOB

The most important thing you will need is a comfortable pair of shoes. Most uniformed jobs require black shoes, no sneakers allowed. I wear boots with my slacks pulled over the shaft, never tucked in or bloused. You do NOT want to cheap out here! Do not buy your shoes at Walmart or Payless or the thrift store. Get the best footware you can afford. Cheap shoes are no bargain when you are on your feet all day, walking over 5 miles per shift. Cheap shoes will not only cause blisters and bunions, but they will need to be replaced every few months as well, whereas a quality pair of shoes will be comfortable to wear and last for years. This is a wise investment.

Next, you will need a decent flashlight. Something small but bright, not a giant Maglite that weighs you down with multiple D-cell batteries and casts a dim light. You want something that has an impact resistant LED bulb and a CR123 battery with a simple tailcap pushbutton switch. Mine typically cost over $50, but you can find something comparable for under $20. It can clip to your pocket or go in a belt pouch. I attach a keyring to mine with my car and house keys.

Gel pens are great, far better than a standard ballpoint. The black Pilot G-2 1.0 is an excellent choice. They make thick, bold black lines and will work on different types and textures of paper, including damp paper. Carry one with a mini spiral notepad that can fit in a pocket.

If you are allowed to carry pepperspray, go with gel or foam, as the liquid stuff can blow back at you in the wind and will contaminate everyone and everything if used indoors. Get a quality brand: Mace,

Fox, Saber... with a flip top cap instead of a safety. The small 2 ounce can is more than sufficient. The large 4 ounce can just makes you look like an asshole. Do not carry a baton, Tazer, or handcuffs unless you are trained and certified in their use, as well as authorized by your employer and the client to carry it. If you injure someone, even in legitimate self defense, with a weapon you are neither certified or authorized to use, you can reasonably expect to be fired, sued, and arrested for criminal charges. You do not need to be certified in the use of pepperspray, as you can do far less damage and the liability is significantly reduced unless you clearly misused it inappropriately.

Get a decent quality touch screen cellphone with a monthly plan for unlimited data. None of this "pre pay by the minute" or "wifi only" bullshit. You will be on your phone a LOT and you will need access to the internet. Many jobs require you to install an app to do your reports and expect updates throughout your shift, all of which can be GPSed to within 5 feet of your position at the moment of upload. You will also likely use your phone to clock in and out, check your paystubs, check emails, look up important phone numbers and addresses, and goof off on your plentiful time off reading eBooks and telling Facebook it is wrong. The phone is your lifeline! Keep it charged, and protect it with an Otter Box or similar protective case. While walking your rounds, tune into the local police scanner feed on broadcastify. This is entertaining, informative, and makes you appear more official to ne'er do wells.

In the event there is no restroom or port-a-john facilities at your site, try to use common sense and be reasonable. Walk behind a dumpster or some bushes to be a good citizen less likely to be reported to the authorities for indecent exposure. Don't piss on the side of the client's building. If you need to take a dump, drive to the nearest supermarket, fast food place, or convenience store... you are entitled to a 30 minute break while on the clock, and this is a reasonable and legitimate reason to be off site briefly. Don't be like the guard who shat in the client's garbage can and caused us to lose a contract, or like the guard who pissed in the same exact spot in a concrete parking garage several times a shift, leaving a salt encrusted puddle in the stairwell that stank to high hell in the Summer. When I worked the parking garage I carried several wide mouthed plastic bottles that I could discard in the trash if used.

Make sure you stay hydrated and awake. Coffee is a diuretic which will dehydrate you if you have too much. Bring bottled water, or Vitamin Water with electrolytes. Bring food that is nutritious and not messy, like ProBars. This one fatass would bring a giant submarine sammich and a gallon bucket of soda, as well as a box of mini chocolate donuts, and smear his greasy fingers all over the workstation... don't be like that guy. Keep your work area clean, even if the mess isn't yours. You will need to interrupt meals if you need to address a situation, which is why security does not need to clock out for lunch breaks because you are "always on the clock." Do not eat food out of the breakroom fridge like a degenerate. If the client provides free coffee, limit yourself to no more than one cup per shift. Don't be like the guy who literally drank a dozen cups a shift, making the client ask our supervisor tell the guards we couldn't drink coffee no more... instead of doing that, he yelled at the dessicated dumbass for embarrassing him as guards need coffee. I would buy 4 packs of those canned Starbucks Espresso Doubleshots, which were a good investment.

Finally, and most importantly, MAKE POSITIVE USE OF YOUR TIME!!! You will likely have an abundance of free time. You can waste it, sitting on your progressively growing ass while stuffing your face with sweets and smoking cigarettes, or you can use the opportunity to get some exercise. At my current site I have access to two different gyms and use both of them every shift. You can also read books or study and do homework for college courses. I have written several books while working graveyard shifts. Instead of watching videos and listening to music on your phone, you can research subjects that interest you or learn new skills. I have known guards who would repair items, tie fishing flies, shoot pellet guns at tin cans... all better than sitting on your fat ass moaning about how miserable you are because you "ruined your life" (like my co-worker, who is such a joy to talk with, let me tell you). Plan a new project, start a new business, blog about something you have expertise in, participate in specialized forums, send emails, search for collectible items that fancy you on eBay, find out of print books on Amazon.

Make good use of your time. An abundance of free time is the BEST thing about security work. Boredom will kill you. Find something fun or productive to pass the time.

As long as you always show up on time, are unfailingly polite to the client and your employer, and do nothing to generate complaints, this is steady work with a regular schedule. The pay is better than most entry level jobs and the work is not very demanding. A lot of retired people and disabled people seek out these jobs. But you need to be okay with working alone, without a need for constant conversation or a tendency to spook at shadows. This is one of the best possible jobs for an introvert or a misanthrope. I highly recommend this career path.

BASIC SECURITY FUNDAMENTALS

CONTENTS

E. REVIEW

F. CONCLUSION

A. INTRODUCTION

Welcome to Training Module I, "Basic Security Fundamentals." This module is intended to instruct entry level guards in the basic expectations of all employees. It will tell you what you need to do in order to perform your job effectively and efficiently, and more importantly it will warn you what NOT to do. This is the introductory training required of all new hires and must be completed prior to any advanced training. Every post will have a unique set of challenges reflected in the post orders. This module is intended to convey only the basics applicable to every post. It does not constitute an all inclusive complete training. Any questions may be addressed by the instructor at the end of each section, please refrain from asking questions until the proper time. Any additional questions may be directed to your supervisor. Let us proceed.

B. ESSENTIAL FUNCTIONS

Security, at the entry level, can be one of the easiest of all jobs, at least 95% of the time; but that other 5% it is very important that the security officer be able to respond to incidents and interact with a variety of persons, including police, emergency services, and representatives of the client, in an efficient and professional manner. This is the greatest challenge for security personnel, where many of them fail.

However, an inferior employee will fail to maintain a minimum standard of performance even during a normal workday when no incidents arise. There are many ways this can occur, and a substandard employee is a serious liability, potentially exposing the company to negative publicity as well as litigation. This training module will address the essential functions of a security officer as well as minimum standards of performance.

While we would all prefer that our employees always perform their duties perfectly, consistently, and enthusiastically, it is understood that this is not always a realistic expectation. Sometimes things happen that are beyond your control, and while we can often make reasonable accommodations with proper notice, a pattern of inconsistency is indicative of a problem employee. What we expect from every employee is at least the bare minimum. While the duties may vary from post to post, the minimum requirements are typically to show up on time, in uniform, clock in, do your assigned rounds, write a shift report, and clock out without causing any problems in the process. Unfortunately, in many cases it seems like this is too much to ask of some people. They expect to be paid and treated the same as everyone else when they show up late, out of uniform, and neglect their assigned duties. This is unacceptable and those problem employees will be weeded out, terminated, and denied unemployment claims due to their conduct. In order to avoid any misunderstandings, this training module is intended to specifically outline our expectations of each employee, as well as address common issues.

B1. ATTENDANCE

All employees are expected to familiarize themselves with the schedule, keep track of which shifts they work, and adhere to it. Employees must arrive at the site at least 5 minutes before their shift begins and remain on site for the full duration of their shift. If an employee is unable to work a shift they must notify a supervisor at least 48 hours in advance so another officer may be scheduled. This is the most basic and essential function of the security officer: arrive for your assigned shift.

Surprisingly, some officers consistently arrive on site late, usually only a few minutes, but in some cases over an hour, and sometimes fail to arrive at all. This is a huge problem and completely unacceptable. If you arrive late, the person you are relieving must stay late, which is inconsiderate and negatively impacts morale. Also, representatives of the client may be at the site awaiting your arrival, and if you fail to show up on time it may result in loss of the contract.

Once you are on site, with very limited and specific exceptions, you are expected to remain on site the entire assigned shift, and if your relief fails to arrive you are expected to notify a supervisor and remain on site until relief arrives. Our primary function is to fulfill the terms of the contract by being on site at the assigned shifts to observe, report, and intervene as necessary. If no-one is on site during an assigned shift we are in breach of contract. Your duty is to perform the task to which you agreed as a condition of your employment.

B2. APPEARANCE

All employees are expected to maintain a professional appearance at all times while on duty. Employees must arrive on site wearing their assigned uniform, which should be clean, complete, and in good repair. If an employee needs uniform components to be issued or replaced it is their responsibility to contact a supervisor. Employees should be neatly groomed and maintain good hygiene. Body language also says a lot, and a guard who is slouching, dragging his feet, and leaning upon fixtures for support will fail to command respect and may instead elicit contempt. An employee's appearance reflects upon the company, positively or negatively.

The uniform tells people who you are. It lets them know that you belong there and have authority granted by the client. If you are not wearing anything identifying you as a security guard people may feel threatened or offended by your approaching them. Similarly, if you are in uniform, but your clothes are disheveled and stained and you have greasy hair and an offensive odor, people will not trust your authority or judgment. If you are neither recognized or respected, at best your presence will be disregarded, at worst it may encourage or provoke an altercation. Employees are expected to present themselves in a professional manner as they are directly representing both the company and the client while they are on site.

B3. ATTITUDE

Of even greater importance than appearance is attitude. A guard can be immaculately dressed in a brand new uniform with polished shoes and excellent posture, but if he is rude to a client's customer or expresses disinterest while performing duties in a lackadaisical manner, there will be complaints and the company may lose the contract. An aggressive or discourteous attitude can also provoke or escalate an altercation, whereas a calm and polite attitude can discourage or de-escalate conflict. Again, body language conveys a lot of messages and it is important to be aware of how you are being perceived by others.

While it is GREAT to take your job seriously and treat even minor tasks with importance, sometimes a guard who strives for perfection can actually be more problematic than a lackadaisical guard who only does the bare minimum. How can this be? Well sometimes too much is as bad as too little. If you overthink things your job will become far more complicated than it needs to be and you will needlessly elevate your own stress levels as well as those of everyone you come into contact with. This is seldom justified. The rules exist for a reason: if you are unsure of what to do, refer to the rules. But common sense is even more important than strict adherence to the rules. Rules are a guide, and they generally apply to 90% of all situations, but they rarely cover everything and occasionally there may be a need for a common sense reinterpretation. Always use common sense and good judgment. Is the rule critical or is it arbitrary? Is there a reasonable cause to make a minor exception? The client expects certain rules to be enforced without exception, but others are a bit more flexible. For example, "Cite everyone in the pool area after 9PM" is a good rule, but you treat a polite family who is found at the pool at 9:05 a bit differently than a group of uncooperative drunks who are causing a disruption after hours at 11PM. Another example is no parking zones. If a car without a parking pass is spotted in a fire lane or handicapped spot at midnight feel free to tow them without notice, but would you yell at a pizza delivery driver with his hazard lights on who "will be back in a minute?" You will probably be meeting that guy again, and there can be complaints from tenants if the pizza place tells them they no longer deliver there because of security. I have actually heard several cases of security guards putting a boot on a running ambulance with emergency lights flashing. That is a huge fine, automatic loss of contract, and probable lawsuit. Use common sense. Remember, you directly represent both your employer and the client. Do not make them look bad due to your attitude.

An additional note for ROVERS who are assigned a marked company vehicle. Please remember that the name of the company is printed in large letters on all sides of that vehicle. Your driving, as well as your interactions with other motorists and pedestrians, will be noted by others, including potential clients. If you are spotted driving carelessly, recklessly, or aggressively some people may feel compelled to complain about it on social media, and when a potential client

Googles our company your bad driving will be addressed. Furthermore, your vehicle can be towed to impound if you park it inappropriately, and if you go through a red light or exceed the speed limit the company may receive a photo ticket which you will be responsible for paying. You also may be held civilly or criminally responsible for any accidents, and that may result in negative publicity. If you are assigned a vehicle please drive it responsibly in a courteous manner, because you are not only representing the company but present a highly visible advertisement. We do not want that message to be, "Don't hire us, we're unprofessional." Be a safe driver.

B4. COMPETENCE

A security officer needs to be able to perform the essential functions of his position, after sufficient training and with reasonable accommodation. If an officer is unable to perform these functions due to ineptitude, incompetence, or disability, then they cannot fulfill the terms of their employment agreement or the company's contract with the client.

Basically, the core fundamentals of the job are very simple: Dress yourself properly, show up on time, perform the minimum site requirements (including site specific special orders), and do not generate complaints from the client regarding attitude or negligence. If you are smart and careful it is a very easy and safe job. If you are stupid and careless it can be very difficult and dangerous.

Competence entails all three prior elements, as well as actual and correct performance of site specific tasks. If a guard has had adequate training, pays attention to detail, and has a modicum of common sense, competence is rarely a problem. Incompetence is usually due to laziness, inattention to detail, or some form of mental defect. Incompetence is an inability to perform the job which cannot be corrected through training or discipline. Fortunately, it is a rare condition. Most guards can easily perform the simple duties assigned to them.

C. DUTIES

The primary functions of the typical security officer are to: establish a presence as a visible deterrent, ensure that doors and gates are secure, and observe and report all suspicious incidents. These are all very simple, yet essential tasks. A few sites will have additional specific instructions per our contract with the client. Furthermore, every security guard is responsible for reporting for duty with a fully charged cellphone and a functional flashlight. Failure to have a cellphone or flashlight on site is negligent. YOUR CELLPHONE RINGER MUST BE TURNED ON DURING THE ENTIRETY OF YOUR SHIFT AND YOU MUST BE ABLE TO ACCEPT INCOMING CALLS. Your supervisor will occasionally attempt to reach you via telephone while you are on duty, and if you fail to answer your phone it may result in a police response. If your phone is switched off or not on your person that constitutes negligence. In the event your phone is inoperable or lost you must contact a supervisor as soon as possible. Other helpful gear includes: a notepad, pen, latex gloves, lockblade knife, and pepperspray. Avoid loading yourself down with excessive gear and resist the temptation to carry unauthorized gear. If it is an unarmed post you should not be carrying a sidearm or Tazer. You are not certified as an armed guard, the client did not request an armed guard (and frequently specifically stated that guards not be armed in the contract), and you are not being paid armed guard wages. If you wish to carry a holstered sidearm on duty you MUST be hired specifically as an armed guard and possess an Armed Guard License which requires a 50 state FBI background check and hours of training including a written exam and range qualification. If you are carrying a firearm on duty without authorization you are in violation of contract and presenting a huge liability for both the company and the client. Don't do it. Pepperspray, Mag Lite, and folding knife do not require authorization as they are defensive rather than offensive. Handcuffs are in a grey area. We are generally not expected to make arrests and if handcuffs are utilized improperly it is extremely easy to accidentally cause severe injury, from fractures, to nerve damage, to loss of circulation, and if you have not been trained and certified in their proper use and were not issued them it could be a huge liability. Handcuff pouches, however, are excellent for carrying notepads, gloves, first aid supplies, and other small gear.

C1. VISIBLE DETERRENT

Most criminals do not want to be seen committing crimes. When you arrive on site in uniform you establish a presence as a witness and identify yourself as an authority figure whose job it is to prevent and report crime. That is why the uniform is so important. Simply being at your assigned post is a huge part of your job. If you are not in uniform you will be viewed as a possible threat. Residents may call law enforcement to report you as being "suspicious" or a "prowler," and anyone you confront will become far more defensive and aggressive. Always wear your assigned uniform on duty. That is half your job. If you are not in uniform you are not doing your job.

C2. SECURING DOORS

At each site, guards are typically responsible for the security of specific doors and gates. These are usually unoccupied management offices and maintenance sheds, as well as locked stairwells and gates. Your job is to check each of these doors to make sure that they are locked and secure. If a door is found unlocked or ajar, briefly inspect the area from the doorway and listen for sounds. If everything seems normal, secure the door and note it in your report. If you are unable to secure a door, notify a supervisor for instructions and note it in your report. Some doors are critical, and you may be expected to remain by that door until after hours maintenance arrives (business office, mailroom, etc). Other doors are less important. If you do not know the difference and it is not addressed in your post orders, call your supervisor.

C3. OBSERVE AND REPORT

Observation is the most important part of your job. You need to maintain situational awareness throughout every shift. This is an acquired skill which not everyone has, and must be developed. It is a skill which will be honed over time and which you will never stop learning. It involves watching and listening for anything out of the ordinary, out of place, unusual. The smell of smoke, an open door, a broken window, yelling, a group of men loitering on the property late at night. Eventually you will learn patterns: tones of voice, facial expressions, gestures, gait, indicative of aggression or deception. This skill will keep you safe, and can get help on the scene sooner rather than too late. A negligent guard will ignore these details and might miss an incident altogether, or fail to pick up on cues that an altercation is about to escalate. Pay attention to details.

Security officers are not police. The typical security job does not regularly involve making arrests. If you see evidence of a crime, or a crime being committed, you are expected to observe the parties involved so that you can provide an accurate description to police. For example: "40 year old white male, 6 ft tall, 200 pounds, brown hair, brown overcoat, blue jeans, white sneakers, appears intoxicated and is cursing at security and refusing to leave the site." You need to be very specific when relaying information to police dispatch and will be asked a number of questions, including some you may not know the answer to. Do your best to remain calm and speak clearly. Afterwards, write the details of the incident in your report.

You will be expected to submit at least one report every shift. Typically a beginning of shift report and an end of shift report, with additional reports for any incidents that occur during your shift. If there is evidence of vandalism, graffiti, or break ins, take photographs to attach to your report and notify police, supervisors, and the client as needed.

C4. INCIDENTS

This is the whole reason clients hire security: to deal with potential incidents. Generally all they want is someone with a cellphone who is willing to stay awake all night and call 911 if there is a problem. That's it, and that is what you are being paid for. Incidents will occasionally occur during your shift, many of which do not involve you directly, some of which may even occur off site. The main thing you need to do is REMAIN CALM, assess the situation, and call for assistance if required. If an incident is occurring off site feel free to call it in, but do not leave your site. Dealing with incidents is beyond the scope of this training module and need to be addressed on an individual basis with common sense and within the specific instructions of your supervisor. If there is smoke indicating a fire, call 911 and request the fire department, it is also important to know the locations of fire extinguishers at your site if needed. If someone is injured, use your judgment as to the best course of action. Is it a resident or is it a mentally ill homeless person under the influence of drugs? Sometimes it is best to call 911 for an ambulance rather than administer first aid yourself, especially if you lack training and proper equipment. If you observe someone breaking window of cars or tagging walls with spraypaint, it often is dangerous to approach the person because they frequently are armed, under the influence of drugs, and aggressive. Call 911 and report the incident, then when you know police are on the way you can shine your light on them from a safe distance away and yell "HEY!" which might scare them off, but there is also a chance they could attack you, which is why it is important to call police first. It is very rare for a security guard to be required to put out a fire, stop bleeding, or arrest a criminal. We are expected to call 911 for those things. If you choose to go above and beyond your assigned duties there is a possibility you may receive a commendation or a promotion, but there is an equal chance that you might be injured or sued. It is a risk to take certain chances, and each incident will need to be judged accordingly. I am in no way telling you to avoid getting involved. For example, if someone collapses in the street and you do not know first aid, you can at least block traffic with your car and put on your hazard lights to prevent them from getting run over. That is just common sense to keep them reasonably safe until the ambulance arrives.

C4a. COMMUNICATING WITH EMERGENCY DISPATCH

This is the most important part of your job. 95% of your time will be routine and rather boring, but the other 5% you will be expected to react to an emergency situation in an efficient and competent manner. You are not a policeman expected to make arrests, you are not a paramedic expected to administer CPR, and you are not a fireman equipped to extinguish burning buildings. All of those tasks are best left to experts with extensive training and official certifications. That is why it is generally best to call those experts directly. Emergency response time in Denver is typically within 5 minutes. ALWAYS call 911 before taking action, NO EXCEPTIONS. You may not have opportunity to make a phone call once you involve yourself and if that option is lost no one is coming to help you. If you need to go above and beyond your assigned duties by intervening in a domestic dispute or rendering aid to an accident victim, you will be negligent if you fail to notify emergency dispatch first. Always call 911 before taking action. This is not only for your safety, but the safety of others, and will protect you legally as well, because if the case goes to court the first question you will be asked is likely to be, "When did you call 911?"

First and foremost, have a phone on your person at all times. The phone should have a charged battery. Even if you have no minutes or the phone service has been disconnected you can still use it to call 911, and often the GPS will show dispatch exactly where you are. Speak calmly and clearly from a position of safety. Out of sight or within your locked car are ideal. If a criminal is within 10 feet of you he can easily wrestle that phone away from you, injuring you in the process.

The first question you will be asked is, "Where is the address of your emergency?" You need to know this. If you are working a post you should know the physical address, or at least the cross streets. Give them as much detail as you can, like "At the pool behind the main office" or "In the dumpster enclosure behind building 2." If you cannot tell them where you are the GPS may be of limited use as that service is often inaccurate or switched off. You will also be asked for your name and phone number. Be certain to say you are a security guard. That will elevate your call in the queue and give you more credibility. If, due to adrenaline, you cannot remember the address or phone number, tell them the name of the post you are at and any nearby landmarks. Unless you are calling from a disconnected phone your number will show up automatically on the dispatcher's screen, often with your name and history of prior 911 calls. Working security you can reasonably expect to make at least one 911 call every month.

Next, you will be asked the nature of the emergency so dispatch can immediately assign it to police, fire, paramedics, or "everyone." Many calls will be assigned to both police and fire. If there is a suspect you need to provide a full description to the best of your ability: gender, race, clothing, approximate age height and weight, if they appear to be drunk/drugged (DK), mentally ill (altered mentation), out of control (excited delerium), or armed (handgun, rifle, machete, knife, bat, stick, rocks, etc), as well as what they are doing, what they said, and where they currently are. Be sure to provide accurate colors of pants, shirt, jacket, hat as that is the main way police will likely identify them. If a vehicle is involved provide make, model, and plate number as well as any identifiers such as stickers, customization, or damage. If it is a medical emergency you will be asked a long series of questions about the patient's condition and possibly even talked through the steps for performing CPR or stopping bleeding. Please be advised that over half of the homeless population are IV drug users, most of whom are positive for HIV and HEP, as well as MRSA, a variety of viral infections, and sometimes TB. You can easily become infected upon contact with their blood or saliva. Keep that in mind and know that you are not obligated to perform CPR on a hobo because some rookie dispatcher is telling you to. If the individual is breathing there is no need for CPR, nor is there a need if they have obviously stopped breathing over an hour ago and are now cold. Keep in mind that everything you say to the dispatcher will be recorded, and they will likely remain on the line until police or EMS arrive on scene. Be certain to complete a detailed incident report and send a copy to the proper email address.

Common non-emergency calls are: "downed party" (unconscious, passed out, sleeping, unresponsive), "unwanted party" (trespasser refusing to leave, drunk and disorderly), "party in distress" (rocking, muttering, crying, yelling, but not presenting an active threat), or "sick case" (complaint of difficulty breathing, stomach pain, limb pain, minor injury). These can all go through the 911 switchboard, you do not need to call the non-emergency number for this. Feel free to visit the broadcastify website to listen to live scanner feeds for Denver and surrounding areas in order to better familiarize yourself with emergency communications.

C4b. USE OF FORCE

It is a common rule of thumb that most physical altercations can be avoided through maintaining proper situational awareness and taking care not to escalate a situation through tone, gesture, or proximity. If you are involved in a physical altercation it is statistically likely due to the fact that you made a mistake. You did not spot the deranged hobo staggering towards you while you were looking at Facebook on your phone. You failed to notice that the trespasser you were confronting was becoming emotionally escalated and reaching in his pocket. You let a stranger approach within 5 feet of you and failed to either extend your hand, move to the side, or say BACK OFF when they closed the distance to 3 feet, then 2 feet. PAY ATTENTION to what the person is doing. Are they angry? Do they appear to be drunk or on drugs? Are they acting in a bizarre manner consistent with mental illness? CAN YOU SEE BOTH OF THEIR HANDS? Are they moving towards you too quickly? Are they approaching too closely? ARE THEY REFUSING TO BACK OFF WHEN ASKED TO DO SO?

Remember, in a situation like this you can never say "please" or refer to them as "sir," as those are placating submissive cues that show weakness. However, you need to take care not to escalate the situation by offending them. Offense usually occurs through perceived "disrespect," often due to the person feeling they were condescended to, mocked, insulted, threatened, or yelled at. Often people are attacked as a direct result of having provoked the other party, sometimes unintentionally. People can be triggered by aggression or humiliation, and the person doing those things often does not realize that their words and tone are triggering a violent reaction and may continue to provoke until violence is inevitable. VIOLENCE CAN USUALLY BE AVOIDED.

As a security guard you are generally expected only to "observe and report," not make arrests. In many cases it is best not even to confront an individual or group that appears escalated and potentially violent. ALWAYS CALL 911 PRIOR TO TAKING ANY ACTION. Maintain a distance of at least 15 feet, retreat or secure yourself in a locked vehicle if necessary for safety. You are neither obligated nor expected to physically engage a trespasser. Confrontations frequently escalate to verbal altercations, which often escalate to physical altercations, which can then escalate very rapidly to attempted homicide. An individual who is unbalanced or impaired can be very unpredictable. Do not engage unless you have no choice. Call 911 and let police handle it. Confronting an aggressor can result in injury and legal liability. Expect anyone you injure to press criminal charges and sue. Avoid physical contact unless absolutely necessary.

Assault is defined simply as: "Intentionally putting another person in reasonable apprehension of an imminent harmful or offensive contact. No intent to cause physical injury needs to exist and no physical injury needs to result. An assault is carried out by a threat of bodily harm coupled with an apparent present ability to cause the harm." Aggravated assault occurs when there is intent to cause physical harm, whereas simple assault only requires the intent to intimidate or frighten. You are being assaulted if an aggressive party states that he intends to do you harm then either closes the distance or places his hand in a pocket. You do not need to wait for him to strike you or draw a weapon to attack. If you are unable to retreat from an aggressor whom you reasonably believe intends to injure you, you are lawfully permitted to defend yourself using the minimum level of force necessary, but you will be required to articulate, in specific detail, exactly why you felt threatened as well as why a lesser use of force was insufficient.

C4b1. PEPPERSPRAY

The security guard's primary weapon is pepperspray. Pepperspray is effective within 10 feet and can keep an aggressor from closing the distance thereby preventing an attack, it also does not result in permanent injury and the effects wear off within an hour. There are many types of spray devices. Foggers must be avoided as they cannot be used indoors or in the wind. Streamers can also cause cross contamination or be effected by wind, but to a lesser degree than foggers. The popular Mace Gun is a type of long distance streamer effective to 15 feet. Cannisters of gel or foam based sprays are designed for indoor use. Remember, after a spray device is used it will begin to lose pressure and should be replaced as soon as possible. In order to use a spray device, aim for the chest and hold the button down, then lift the stream into the face, continuing to fire until the aggressor stops advancing. Usually a 3 second squirt will be sufficient, but often an aggressor will choose to continue their attack in which case you need to continue firing until the device is empty. Pepperspray causes inflammation which impairs vision and breathing, providing opportunity to retreat. It will not always be effective, especially against an individual impaired by drugs or highly motivated to hurt you, so be aware that it is not a magic wand, simply a tool. Feel free to use pepperspray whenever you are threatened by someone who appears to have the ability and motivation to hurt you. Feel free to use it against aggressive dogs. NEVER use pepperspray against an individual who does not appear to have the means to injure you, such as a drunk yelling insults from a park bench or a 12 year old child. If you cannot articulate why use of force was necessary you will be guilty of a crime and the company and client can be sued. All weapons are a potential liability, but pepperspray is less of a liability than any other option, which is why we issue it. If you are uncomfortable with the bulk or configuration of a Mace Gun feel free to purchase a more traditional cannister, preferably with a flip-top instead of a safety switch. ABSOLUTELY NO FOGGERS PERMITTED. Foggers are ineffective in wind, have unacceptable levels of cross contamination, and can never be used indoors. Only streamers, gel, and foam are suitable.

C4b2. MAG-LITE

Another common choice of weapon for security guards is the clubbed flashlight, such as the aluminum Mag-Lite. Flashlights are legal to carry whereas batons are not, but they can do even more damage than a baton, potentially breaking bones with every strike. A blow to the head is frequently fatal. Police are permitted to utilize batons and flashlights a variety of ways, but we are not police. Strikes with the Mag-Lite must be limited to strictly defensive use. Absolutely no strikes to the head, face, neck, or spine are ever permitted. Strikes with the Mag-Lite must be limited only to an attacker's hands, elbows, and arms, to deter him from striking or grabbing you. That way you can claim you were blocking rather than attacking and cannot be held criminally or civilly liable.

Absolutely no firearms or Tazers permitted on site unless you are certified and authorized by your employer to carry same. No exceptions.

D. PROBLEMS

Most problems on a site are the result of a guard failing to perform at the minimum expected standards. For examples, by failing to be present on post when an incident occurs, by confronting a trespasser while out of uniform or in a rude and unprofessional manner, by sleeping on duty, or by making serious errors which create problems and complaints. If you are alert, diligent, and use good judgment you will have relatively few problems. Your primary function is simply to observe and report. Security guards are not policemen. Your lawful authority and power of arrest is very limited, and if you overstep your authority it can result in lawsuits, criminal charges, and negative publicity for the company.

D1. MINOR DISCREPANCIES

Security guards are human, and it is human nature to occasionally make mistakes. No-one is perfect. Most minor errors are not even noticed by the client. If, for example, you are expected to patrol the grounds every hour of an 8 hour shift but only make 6 patrols because it is raining, that is understandable. However, if you are questioned about an error you may have made, it is best to admit that you failed to patrol a certain area rather than lie about it, because we will need to determine an accurate timeline. Also, if you are ever asked a question to which you do not know the answer, it is best to say, "I don't know, but I will try to find the answer for you," rather than guessing and making something up. Minor errors are expected and forgivable, but can become major errors if they become a pattern of laziness or you attempt to cover them up through deceit. Common discrepancies include: forgetting to clock in or out, forgetting to post a report, arriving on site no more than 15 minutes late. If ANY of these discrepancies occur, immediately contact a supervisor for assistance.

D2. INCOMPETENCE

Incompetence occurs when a guard attempts in good faith to correctly execute the duties of his position but makes errors due to ineptitude, ignorance, poor judgment, or bad time management skills. At best, the guard bumbles his way through the shift, working a lot harder than he should because he needs to backtrack or redo tasks. At its worst, it constitutes negligence, which is grounds for termination, because the guard failed to perform an essential task properly and an incident occurred as a direct result. Usually incompetence is the result of poor training and unclear instructions, which is not necessarily the guard's fault. Pay attention during training and ask questions. If, during your shift, you ever have a question about how to deal with a problem that is not addressed in the site specific post orders, feel free to call a supervisor or dispatch to request instructions. Incompetence can generally be prevented through proper training and adequate oversight. However, on rare occasions there will be an employee who proves themselves untrainable. This is typically noted very early, as the trainee fails to pay attention to the trainer and often will talk over the trainer or be insubordinate by indicating they do not wish to follow instructions because they feel "their way is better" or they resent being told what to do. This is often due to a personality disorder or some sort of mental defect. If, after repeated attempts at training the behaviors persist and tasks are still not being performed properly, then the employee will be deemed a liability and will be terminated.

D3. NEGLIGENCE

Negligence occurs when a guard arrives on site, in uniform, but fails to perform assigned duties due to laziness. The most common complaint regarding security officers working overnight shifts is that of sleeping on duty. Many dishonest people seek out security jobs as a way of making easy money for being paid to sleep, and will sleep for hours every shift, whereas the average employee will only fall asleep if they are sick, overtired from another job, or simply bored. You are not being paid to sleep on duty. You are being paid to watch over the client's property, and if you are sleeping you are failing to perform at the minimum standards. Crimes can occur while you are asleep, or a resident could be injured and in need of help but you would not notice it and the next day the client will ask, "where was the security I was paying for?" Or, a representative of the client could see you sleeping, take your photograph, and ask the company why they are not receiving the service they paid for. That usually results in either an immediate loss of contract, or a demand for new guards and a month of free service which puts a significant financial strain on the company.

Another common form of negligence is failure to do assigned patrols. If you are expected to perform an hourly foot patrol of the perimeter but miss one, that does not constitute negligence. Negligence is when you do a single patrol at the beginning of your shift then spend the rest of your time in your car using an electronic device to play games, watch movies, or chat on Facebook. It is fine to do that occasionally throughout the night to help you stay awake, but some people become so absorbed in what they are doing, particularly if their windows are up and they are using earphones, that they might fail to notice a crime occurring right in front of them. And then, at the end of their shift, they type "no incidents" into their report when a unit has a door hanging off its hinges due to a break in and there is fresh graffiti on the management office. You will be held accountable for reporting every incident that occurs on your shift, and if you are lazy or distracted you may fail to even notice that an incident has occurred. This constitutes negligence, which is grounds for termination as well as the possibility of civil damages.

D4. DERELICTION

Dereliction of Duty is a very serious offense. In fact, the military considers it so serious that it can result in imprisonment and a dishonorable discharge. There are many forms of dereliction, but the two most common ones are being absent from a post without leave, or being intoxicated on duty.

Generally, with very few specific exceptions, once you arrive on post you are expected to remain there for the duration of your shift. However, if no restroom facilities are provided you are typically allowed to drive to a convenience store to use the restroom there. Similarly, if you forgot to bring a lunch you might be permitted to go through a nearby drive-thru or get a cup of coffee provided you return to site immediately. Driving to your preferred restaurant 5 miles away and having dinner at a table for an hour would be considered dereliction. However, most cases of dereliction are actually far worse than that. Typically the guard arrives on site to clock in, leaves, then returns at the end of shift to clock out. Or they may even clock in and out without even bothering to arrive on site at all. Not only is this grossly negligent, but it is a deliberate and premeditated act of theft. You are wrongfully and unlawfully taking payment for a service you have willfully decided not to provide, thereby defrauding both the company and the client. This frequently results in not only termination but being personally sued for the return of wages paid under false pretenses and damages as a result of loss of contract. It is a criminal act that is usually settled in civil court.

Fortunately, intoxication is not a common problem, but occasionally an employee presents with a substance abuse problem which results in him reporting for duty under the influence of alcohol. If you consumed a single beer several hours prior, that is a non issue, but arriving with a BAC above the legal limit certainly is, especially if you intend to drive a company vehicle. Marijuana is legal in Colorado and can have psychoactive effects which last for many hours that can result in impaired judgment or an inability to perform assigned tasks. To someone, such as a police officer or substance abuse counselor, a person under the influence of alcohol or marijuana is very obvious, especially if their abilities are significantly impaired. No-one under the influence of alcohol or marijuana has any business driving a car or confronting people under color of authority as either could have severe and tragic results, although most frequently such a person chooses to neglect their duties rather than attempt to perform them. Other unlawful drugs, as well as misused prescription medication, have not been addressed as it would be redundant and beyond the scope of this module. Reporting under the influence of drugs or alcohol is grounds for immediate termination.

D5. MISCONDUCT

Misconduct is the most serious of all offenses, as it involves a prosecutable criminal act such as: battery, theft, or sexual assault. As with any crime, there are levels of severity, largely dependent upon intent and damage. Battery is the most frequent accusation made against security officers. Under certain, very limited, circumstances, a guard has lawful right to place their hands upon another person: to protect themselves from unlawful attack, to stop an unlawful attack against another person on site, or to detain the individual for citizen's arrest pending arrival of law enforcement. You are not permitted to maliciously beat someone who presents no viable physical threat to yourself or others. If a drunk is walking through the parking lot cursing at people then urinates on a wall, you cannot bludgeon, Mace, or Tazer him simply for being offensive. That is a felony, you will go to jail, and the company as well as the client can be sued by the victim. If you are patrolling a residential community and note that a door is ajar, you are typically not lawfully permitted to enter that unit without permission from the resident or client barring what is known as "exigent circumstances," defined as hearing screams for help or the sounds of physical violence therein, and even then it is always best to remain outside the unit and call 911 for police to respond rather than entering yourself. You are not police. Your authority is typically limited only to reporting crimes which you observe. You are not trained how to intervene in a domestic violence situation or put handcuffs on a non-compliant individual without seriously injuring them. And the very act of entering an occupied unit constitutes misdemeanor criminal trespass which could rapidly escalate to multiple felonies if you were attacked by a frightened resident and attempted to defend yourself. Familiarize yourself with the many legal limitations on your behavior as a guard. With the exception of pepperspray or a small folding knife, if you are not issued a weapon you should not have a weapon in your possession, even if you have a permit to carry same. That presents a huge liability to the company. The same thing goes for handcuffs, if you have not been trained and certified there is a very high risk that you could seriously injure someone while attempting to cuff them, resulting in the company being sued. But these are both cases in which a guard exceeded his authority without actual criminal intent. Often misconduct is much worse.

Whenever something is stolen from a site, the first suspect is usually the security guard, because it is a low paying, entry level, unskilled job given to a person who has unrestricted access to the property in the middle of the night. It is very easy for a dishonest guard to steal, so the guard will be looked at first before deciding it was a random criminal passing through. Your integrity must be beyond question to eliminate unwarranted suspicion. Sometimes very expensive equipment or a vehicle is stolen from a secure building, and it is obvious that only an employee or contractor would have known where it was, and the guard is one of the few people with access. If a client's employee is dishonest, they will often try to shift the blame for their thefts to the guard. You need to be careful of this.

This is a difficult subject to address, but when an abduction of a woman or child takes place, and the perpetrator is unknown, detectives will often consider local security guards as potential suspects. That is because deranged persons who long to have power over others, but cannot pass the psychological examination necessary to become a police officer, are often attracted to security positions. They get to wear a uniform with a badge, may drive a vehicle that looks similar to a police car, and have authority to issue commands to others within limitations. A deranged person will disregard those limitations and outright impersonate a policeman, even going so far as to pull over vehicles on the highway and unlawfully detain people. Even if the person is never taken from the location, the simple act of preventing them from leaving constitutes felony kidnapping. In Denver alone, there are an average of two dozen reports of police impersonators every year, most of which turn out to be security guards. Remember, you have zero authority off site, you cannot lawfully perform security duties off site, and you certainly cannot pull people over for traffic offenses. If you need to confront a female or a child, it is important to call 911 to have a police response. False accusations of sexual harassment or assault against guards, police, and other authority figures are not uncommon, and if you do not have a body cam or a surveillance camera in the vicinity it will be your word against theirs. Your first priority is always your own safety, followed by the assigned duties. If you feel there is a situation that needs to be intervened in, but you do not feel comfortable confronting the person alone without witnesses, call the police rather than risk a malicious accusation.

Fortunately, criminal misconduct amongst security guards is rare, but accusations of theft and sexual harassment are not uncommon, and they can prove a huge liability to the company. If your appearance and conduct are always professional it is far less likely that a false accusation will be viewed by the client as credible.

E. REVIEW

In review, what we have learned is the importance of adhering to the basic core expectations of an entry level security guard. First and foremost, ATTENDENCE, showing up for your assigned shifts on time and clocking in. Second, APPEARANCE, arriving for duty in uniform with a squared away appearance. Third, ATTITUDE, remember that you are directly representing both the client and the company. Do not present as lazy and disinterested, nor should you present as rude, condescending, or hostile. Always be alert, professional, and polite. COMPETANCE is satisfactory completion of your assigned duties which include: MANTAINING A VISUAL DETERRANT, SECURING DOORS, and OBSERVE AND REPORT, as well as having a cellphone and flashlight on your person at all times. Remember, you are not a policeman or a paramedic. If an arrest needs to be made or emergency first aid is required, IMMEDIATELY CALL 911 before taking any further action. Always be certain to clock in and out for your shifts and log a daily report. Always be ready to answer your phone or call 911. Those are the bare minimum expectations of every guard.

F. CONCLUSION

This module encompassed the very basic bare minimum requirements of being a security guard. Surprisingly, many guards, including some who have worked for years, are unaware of these fundamentals as it is rare for entry level guards to receive any training whatsoever. If you have any questions you are encouraged to contact your supervisor. You are further advised to seek additional training on the topics of fire safety, first aid, and conflict management. Thank you for your participation in this training.

Made in the USA
Columbia, SC
29 February 2024

32481771R00026